365

CONNECTING QUESTIONS
for COUPLES

REVISED AND UPDATED

365

CONNECTING
QUESTIONS
for COUPLES

REVISED AND **UPDATED**

. . .

WITH **200** NEW QUESTIONS

CASEY AND **MEYGAN CASTON**

CONVERGENT

New York

Published in the United States by Convergent Books,
an imprint of Random House, a division of Penguin
Random House LLC, New York.

CONVERGENT BOOKS is a registered trademark and
the Convergent colophon is a trademark of
Penguin Random House LLC.

Originally self-published by the authors in different form
in 2018.

ISBN 9780593736388
Ebook ISBN 9780593736395

Printed in the United States of America on
acid-free paper

convergentbooks.com

2 4 6 8 9 7 5 3 1

Book design by Simon M. Sullivan

DEDICATION

To our incredible Marriage365 community. Your unwavering support, encouragement, and belief in our journey are the foundation on which this book stands.

Thank you for being our constant source of inspiration and strength, and for trusting us with your relationship.

CONTENTS

INTRODUCTION TO THE NEW EDITION

• • •

IT ALL STARTED WITH A QUESTION.

"Hi, what's your name?" a cute guy asked me at a coffee shop one random day twenty-three years ago. "I'm Casey."

One question led to another, and we ended up chatting for a while that evening. There was instant chemistry. You know the feeling—butterflies in your stomach, heart all aflutter, can't-take-your-eyes-off-each-other kind of excitement. We both fell hard and started dating shortly after.

I still remember those dating years and how easy it was to spend hours lost in conversation. I wanted to know everything about Casey. Where he grew up, what his family was like, what his career aspirations were. I even wanted to know silly things like how he found out there was no Santa Claus. He could hardly give a wrong answer; I found each one fascinating. There's nothing like that rush of early love when you're eager to learn everything about someone you adore.

Less than two years later, we were married. Days turned into months turned into years, and things changed. Going into this, we were just about as unprepared as you can be to create a successful marriage. Between our sets of parents, there are twelve marriages, so we never had a model of what it takes for a relationship to last. We didn't have good financial habits, either. Casey and I both hid purchases from each other and racked up over $250,000 worth of debt in just those first few years. Casey also had some traditional ideas of what kind of wife I'd be—cooking, cleaning, homemaking—because that was the kind of household he grew up in. But I don't like to cook and always wanted to work outside of the home. Not to mention the fact that we're both strong-willed, stubborn, and natural-born leaders, so there was hardly a topic we didn't clash over. We fought over everything from our careers down to what was for dinner. Every. Single. Day.

We had zero conflict-resolution skills and both of us were dead set on trying to be right. Over time, we stopped going on dates. We stopped being curious about each other. Because almost every interaction led to a conflict, we hardly spoke at all. We didn't ask each other about our childhoods anymore or know what the other's goals were last month. And in the absence of meaningful connection, we grew apart. We were on the verge of divorce. There was so much hurt and distance that it seemed impossible to bring back the passion and romance we once had. Neither of us had any idea how to fix our relationship. We felt like two battle-worn combatants, exhausted from the war and helpless to do anything to get out of it. We didn't want to fight anymore, but we couldn't see our way back to each other.

One day, in the depths of the worst of it, I was sitting on my therapist's couch alone because Casey wouldn't go with me. I admitted I was thinking of leaving, and she let me rant for over an hour about everything that was wrong before she finally asked me, "Have you done anything and everything you can do to work on your marriage so you don't live with regret?"

A good question.

The honest answer was no. I was mainly waiting for Casey to fall to his knees, beg me for forgiveness, and admit that it was all his fault. (That'd be nice, right? Not how it usually goes, unfortunately.)

"Well," she continued, "creating a better marriage starts with creating a better you. You can't control Casey or his actions, words, tone, or motivations. But you can control yours." That sparked something in me. It forced me to evaluate myself and how I showed up as a partner. For the first time, I didn't feel so helpless. I had agency. I decided right then to focus on what I could control so that no matter what happened to our marriage over the next year, I could be proud of who I was and how I handled it. I was dedicated to becoming the healthiest partner I could be.

My therapist began to walk me through a series of steps that focused on my own growth. The first of the steps was this . . .

Ask Him a Question.

But not just any kind of question—an open-ended question designed to get him talking. "Start a conversation that doesn't center around the necessary logistics of your life or a topic that you know will trigger a fight," she said. Not an especially easy thing for me to do back then. She explained that it's normal for couples to fall into a communication rut after some time together. I'd call it more of a chasm than a rut . . . but fine, I'd try it. I had decided on that first day of therapy sitting on that couch that I was all in. I knew that the best version of myself would initiate that kind of connecting conversation, and I wanted to be that person.

My homework was to get curious about Casey again, like I'd been in those early days of dating. I wasn't supposed to start with anything too deep or personal just yet, because we had destroyed any trust or emotional safety over the last three years with our bickering. I would ask him a question about something other than the boring, mundane, daily things we were used to talking about.

So one night at dinner, I looked across the table and asked, "What was your bedroom like as a teenager?" Casey looked a little stunned. It had been such a long time since we had a real conversation that he hardly seemed to know how to answer. Plus, it was a little random.

"Um, well, I was a big aviation nerd," he replied. "I hung little model airplanes from my ceiling with fishing wire and had a huge poster of a cockpit on my wall." I never knew that about him. We smiled across the table at each other. For the first time in a long time, we felt connected. Day by day, I started to ask him short, thought-provoking questions like these: *What did you want to be as a child? What would you do if you won a million dollars? What was the most memorable gift you ever received?*

And you know what? It worked! Slowly but surely, over the course of many months, we actually started to talk again. I began to remember who he was and why I loved him so much. When I listened closely and leaned into what he shared, he felt safe, known, and cared for, which led him to ask me questions in return. I felt like I'd unlocked some secret to relationships that no one had ever explained before.

Over the next few years, we were able to turn our marriage around completely. Though there were many different things we did to help heal our relationship, I can tell you with 100 percent certainty that what helped the most was regularly asking each other open-ended questions. It helped us fall back in love and has continued to grow that love every day since. Back then, we didn't really know what we were doing; we just knew that it was working.

Today, thanks to recent studies and research, we know that we were engaging in one of the best-known ways to create connection and heal loneliness: asking intentional, open-ended questions to spark insightful, personal conversation. We are all wired for connection. One of the greatest joys of life is knowing someone deeply and letting them know you. Since at least the beginning of recorded history, we've tribed up and done everything in community, starting with our closest, committed relationships. But it's so easy to fall into the pattern that Casey and I did—only having conversations centered on schedules, meals, kids, bills, etc. Before you know it, you look across the table and realize you hardly know each other anymore.

We are living in the midst of a loneliness epidemic. Though we're more connected than ever because of the internet and social media, technology has made it easy to disconnect from real relationships, even the most meaningful one right in front of you. If you've picked up this book, you might understand what it's like to feel lonely in your own house with the person or people who love you the most. Let's fix that.

The best way to heal loneliness and build emotional intimacy is by asking open-ended questions.

Having a hard day? Ask a fun question.

Looking for more depth in a conversation? Ask a self-awareness question.

Want to spice things up in the bedroom? Ask a sexy question.

Having a fun day and want to connect? Ask a light-hearted question.

Getting to know someone new? Ask a childhood question.

Organizing your finances? Ask a money question.

Hurting in your relationship? Ask a repairing question.

This concept worked so well for Casey and me that we began coaching other couples through their relationship conflicts, too. We created a whole movement and app called Marriage365 to help couples engage in better question asking. Like us, we saw that the majority of couples really want to connect and have healthy and interesting conversations but feel lost and confused about how to start. Do we need to say it again? Ask a question!

Six years ago, we created a book that gave couples a year's worth of open-ended questions. They were the questions that changed everything for us, and hundreds of thousands of other couples around the world. We've heard from newlyweds who were given the book as a wedding gift say the questions gave them a strong foundation for their happily ever after. We've heard from couples who are in the busy parenting stage of life finally reconnecting in just five minutes with a question a day. And, most miraculously of all, we've heard from separated couples on the brink of breaking up who healed their relationships.

The response has been incredible. We learned so much along the way about what kinds of questions sparked the best conversations. Some of the questions were clearly fan favorites. Many readers told us there were topics we hadn't covered, like mental health, career, and emotional connection, that they wished were in the book. We also learned which questions felt alienating or hard to answer. And so we took all of that feedback and created this revised edition.

One of the coolest responses we heard regularly was that people were using the questions as journal prompts, so we've added plenty of self-discovery questions, too. While the goal of the original book was to help married couples, we heard from so many readers in different kinds of relationships who loved it that we broadened the scope to include any type of partnership looking to deepen their connection. In total, there are 200 new or revised questions based on the feedback of over one hundred thousand readers, making this book the best it's ever been.

No matter if you're in the early stages of a relationship or have been at it for fifty-plus years, this book can change everything. The magic happens when the power of these connecting questions combines with your effort and care. Many of the questions may seem just for fun, but the purpose is anything but. Take this seriously. Your relationship may depend on it.

So now, let us ask *you* a question: What would your relationship look like a year from now if every day, for just a few minutes, you and your partner had meaningful, funny, eye-opening, and "aha" conversations about all sorts of things? We can guarantee that you will see a positive change in your relationship and experience a true, life-changing connection. All you have to do is open this book once a day for a year. Sounds amazing, right? This might just be the fun-nest and easiest relationship homework you ever get.

Last question: Are you ready? We can't wait to see how these connecting questions help create the kind of relationship you long for. All you have to do is pick a page, any page, and ask a question.

Rooting for you,
Casey and Meygan

HOW AND WHEN TO USE THIS BOOK

By date: For each day of the year, there is one connecting question. Turn to the date of the year and take turns asking the question listed. You can start at any day of the year.

By topic: If there is a specific topic you want to discuss, pick a question by topic using the list of topics on page xxv.

Topics
Boundaries
Childhood
Communication
Conflict and Repair
Friendship and Romance
Holidays and Celebrations
Just for Fun
Mental Health
Money
Roles, Career, and Household Chores
Self-discovery
Sex and Intimacy

Plus over one hundred bonus questions about parenting and faith

When to Use This Book
- At dinner
- In the car
- On your date night

- Over the phone
- During a weekend getaway
- On the couch after the kids go to bed
- Right before you go to bed
- While taking a walk
- As a text or email if you're spending a long time apart

Tips for Making the Most of Your Connecting Conversations

1. Limit distractions. Make sure you silence your phones, turn off the TV, put the kids to bed, and are ready to give 100 percent of your time and attention to the conversation.

2. Watch your body language. Remember that 90 percent of communication is nonverbal. Be conscious of your tone, attitude, eye contact, and body posture. Use physical touch (hold hands, touch your partner's leg, place your hand on their back) to show that you are invested in what your partner is sharing.

3. Listen with empathy. Empathy means feeling "with" someone, so this means that you need to lean in, listen to understand your spouse's perspective, and allow them to be messy and vulnerable. Stay out of judgment and try not to fix, correct, or minimize what they share.

4. Keep an open mind. Shocker: your spouse thinks differently from you! In order to understand each other, you will need to try seeing things from your spouse's perspective. Be prepared that your spouse might say something that will surprise or even disappoint you. Having an open mind will allow you to learn new things and remember that it doesn't mean you have to agree with them.

5. Don't interrupt. Interrupting sends a variety of messages, like "I'm more important than you," "I don't have time for your opinion," "I don't really care what you think," or "What I have to say is more interesting." If you are truly listening to understand your spouse, you will need a moment to process. It may feel uncomfortable at first, but allow space for silence, giving you both time to reflect and form your thoughts.

6. Watch out for triggers. If your marriage has been on autopilot for a while, some of these questions might bring up underlying issues that you've been avoiding or minimizing. Triggers are a warning sign that this topic needs to be worked through. How do you know if you're triggered? Your heart starts to beat faster, your cheeks get flushed, you feel anxious, angry, frustrated, or even disappointed. Take a quick time-out and go for a walk, take a shower, do some yoga—anything that will help restore a calm state before you come back to the conversation. If you can't work through it on your own, it's okay to seek counsel from a therapist to help guide you both through it.

7. Ask clarifying questions. If something your spouse shares causes confusion or they are having difficulty finding the right words, use these clarifying questions.

How did that make you feel?
Why do you think that is?
Can you help me understand what you're trying to say?
Could you repeat that again? I want to make sure I understand you.

8. Don't be too serious! While some of the questions in the book will dig deep into core memories and topics you may have been avoiding, many of the questions are fun and lighthearted and should cause some good laughter. The entire purpose of the book is to connect with each other, and if that's not happening, put the book down and try again tomorrow.

Help! My partner won't read the book with me!

The reality is that your partner may feel threatened, anxious, or nervous about diving into conversations about your relationship, especially if you've been avoiding these kinds of conversations recently. Don't let that stop you from making the most of this book.

Our suggestion is to glance at the question for the day, try your best to memorize it, and casually ask it over dinner or in bed at night. Your partner won't even know where you got the question from and they'll most likely be up for having a casual conversation with you. You can also use the questions as journal prompts to build more self-awareness and grow more in your confidence.

Help! My partner replies "I don't know" to every question!

It may be true. They may have no idea how to answer the question asked. Or maybe they are worried they will look stupid or selfish. Or maybe they don't even know how to process their thoughts and feelings in a healthy way.

The best thing you can do is to be encouraging and positive and say, "That's okay. Why don't you take some time and think about it for a day or two and get back to me. I really want to hear your thoughts on this." And then follow up over the next couple of days. Most people open up when they feel safe and supported, so be patient and don't give up.

Below is a list of feelings to help you and your partner answer the questions in a more thoughtful way when you're stuck.

Feelings Words List

Most of us use the same five emotions when we talk about our experiences. It's time to expand your vocabulary. Use the words below to communicate your feelings more clearly.

loved — romantic — appreciative — refreshed — comforted

peaceful — relieved — safe — relaxed — protected

confident — secure — positive — assertive — self-assured

happy — elated — joyful — satisfied — optimistic — delighted

excited — playful — determined — talkative — rejuvenated

ashamed — guilty — embarrassed — stupid — exposed

sad — hopeless — unhappy — crushed — desperate

anxious — uneasy — worried — fearful — indecisive

alone — abandoned — isolated — disconnected

angry — controlled — grumpy — irritated — bitter

confused — misunderstood — deceived — skeptical

exhausted — depressed — withdrawn — lazy — beaten down

overwhelmed — burdened — guarded — tense — confused

Phrases That Express Empathy

An important part of the process of question asking is responding in an engaging way after your partner has finished. That doesn't come naturally to all of us, especially if you've felt disconnected for some time now. Below is a list of responses you can use to express empathy, especially after your partner has answered one of the harder, deeper questions.

I understand how you're feeling.
How disappointing.
This makes sense.
You must feel so helpless.
I'm on your team, babe.
That would hurt my feelings too.
Tell me more.
I agree 100 percent.
I think you're right.
That would make me mad too.
I'm on your side here.
So what you're saying is . . .

QUESTIONS BY TOPIC

Each question is tagged in one of these categories.

Boundaries
January 4, 15, 21
February 15
March 1, 21
May 22
June 13
July 5
August 11, 26
September 8, 26
October 23
November 12
December 11

Childhood
January 1, 5, 22
February 5, 13
March 5, 11, 23
April 6, 10, 22
May 2, 18
June 8, 15
July 5, 10, 21, 25
August 15, 30
September 10, 22
October 8, 28, 31

November 7, 26, 27
December 18, 21, 28

Communication
January 7, 9, 11
February 12, 18, 26
March 4, 9, 17, 22
April 2, 8, 21
May 1, 17
June 9
July 13, 24
August 8, 25
September 13, 15
October 1, 24, 26
November 19, 22
December 9, 12, 26

Conflict and Repair
January 9, 16
February 11, 23
March 7, 17, 26
April 4, 18, 30
May 6, 23
June 1, 20
July 9, 28
August 1, 18
September 3, 19
October 15, 24
November 3, 30
December 14, 26

Friendship and Romance
January 2, 17, 26
February 14, 19, 24
March 18, 22, 30
April 13, 25
May 13, 28
June 14, 19
July 2, 20
August 6, 14, 17, 23, 27
September 5, 30
October 10, 12, 18
November 11, 14
December 3, 7, 16, 22

Holidays and Celebrations
February 2
May 28, 31
June 22
August 17
October 31
November 2, 8, 18, 24
December 1, 8, 13, 18, 23, 30

Just for Fun
January 1, 19, 27
February 8, 21, 28, 29
March 2, 13, 16
April 14, 23, 27
May 9, 16, 30
June 12, 18, 28
July 4, 14, 17, 19, 31
August 10, 19, 21
September 1, 16, 18, 20, 29

Roles, Career, and Household Chores

January 13, 30
February 7
March 8
April 9
May 10
June 5, 11
July 18
August 4, 22
September 4, 14
October 4, 14
November 10, 20
December 17

Self-discovery

January 3, 8, 14, 20, 24, 28, 31
February 4, 8, 9, 12, 16, 25
March 3, 6, 10, 15, 19, 24, 28
April 1, 3, 7, 8, 11, 16, 20, 24, 29
May 3, 7, 8, 11, 15, 19, 24, 26, 29
June 2, 6, 11, 16, 21, 25, 27, 30
July 1, 6, 11, 16, 22, 26, 30
August 3, 7, 12, 16, 20, 25, 29
September 2, 6, 12, 17, 21, 25, 28
October 2, 6, 11, 16, 20, 25, 30
November 5, 13, 23, 28
December 5, 10, 27, 31

Sex and Intimacy

January 10, 18, 29
February 3, 10, 17, 27
March 4, 12, 20, 25, 31
April 5, 12, 19, 26

May 5, 12, 21, 27
June 3, 10, 17, 24, 29
July 3, 12, 21, 23, 29
August 9, 31
September 7, 24
October 19, 29
November 9, 17
December 6, 19

1

JANUARY

· · ·

If you want to make a better relationship, it starts by making a better you.

JANUARY

1
...

What was your bedroom like when you were
a teenager?

JANUARY

2
...

What made you agree to go on our first date?

JANUARY

3
...

Which of your friends is the most opinionated?
Do you butt heads with them, or do you enjoy
hearing their opinion?

JANUARY

4

...

What sort of boundaries should all couples have
to protect their relationship from infidelity?
Why do you believe those are important?

JANUARY

5

...

Who is someone from your childhood that
showed you a lot of love? What is an example of
what they did that made you feel loved by
them?

JANUARY

6

...

What does self-care look like to you? How well
do you implement self-care into your life?

JANUARY

7

. . .

What's an area in our relationship where there's been a lot of communication but no plan to move forward or follow through? Do you think we're ready to create the next steps? Why or why not?

JANUARY

8

. . .

Do you consider yourself a patient person most of the time, sometimes, or rarely? When do you feel the most impatient?

JANUARY

9

. . .

How can we make sure we are treating each other with respect even during disagreements?

JANUARY

10

...

What does our ideal sex life look like for you in
this season of life?

JANUARY

11

...

Do you feel comfortable asking me for help
when you're unsure of something? Why or why
not?

JANUARY

12

...

Do you think that money can buy you
happiness? Why or why not?

JANUARY

13

...

Do you feel like we are a team when it comes to
making decisions? Why or why not?

JANUARY

14

...

Do you think that having a shared sense of
humor is essential to having a healthy
relationship? Why or why not?

JANUARY

15

...

What is something, or someone, that has taken
up too much of your energy? How could you
change that?

JANUARY
16
...

What do you think it means to be a trustworthy
partner?

JANUARY
17
...

What are some ways we can support and
encourage each other's hobbies and interests?

JANUARY
18
...

How can we romance each other during the day
in anticipation of sex?

JANUARY
19
...

What is your favorite way to spend the
weekend?

JANUARY
20
...

Which of your five senses do you think is the
strongest? Why do you think that?

JANUARY
21
...

What are boundaries that we need to set up to
protect ourselves from unhealthy family
members and friends?

JANUARY

22

...

Did your parents ever show favoritism with your siblings or other family members? Why or why not?

JANUARY

23

...

What activity in your life brings you joy? Why?

JANUARY

24

...

If I spent a typical day in your shoes, what would I experience?

JANUARY

25

...

What are some areas we can improve when it comes to managing our money?

JANUARY

26

...

What are some things I can do to help draw out the funny, goofy, and playful parts of you?

JANUARY

27

...

If you had to teach something, what would you teach and why?

JANUARY

28

· · ·

What is the best and worst thing about getting older?

JANUARY

29

· · ·

Do you prefer sex to be wilder, gentler, or more romantic and why?

JANUARY

30

· · ·

What is one chore you hate doing and would like to outsource?

31

...

Do you consider yourself someone who is intimidating? Why or why not?

FEBRUARY

2

Never forget that you're on the same team, wanting to connect with each other on a deeper level.

FEBRUARY

1
...

What do you think our number-one financial
priority should be this month and why?

FEBRUARY

2
...

What are your expectations for how we spend
Valentine's Day?

FEBRUARY

3
...

Would you ever be open to making love in the
shower? Why or why not?

FEBRUARY

4

. . .

Do you think it's okay to break the law if there
are extenuating circumstances? Why or
why not?

FEBRUARY

5

. . .

What is one thing you experienced in your
childhood that has impacted who you are
today?

FEBRUARY

6

. . .

What are your views about journaling as a way
to process your thoughts, feelings, and
memories?

FEBRUARY

7

...

Do you prefer running errands together, on
your own, or a little of both?

FEBRUARY

8

...

In what ways do you consider yourself to be
unique?

FEBRUARY

9

...

What do you think is the biggest mistake dating
couples make and why?

FEBRUARY

10

...

Think about our first sexual experience together. What are some feelings and thoughts that come to your mind?

FEBRUARY

11

...

When conflict arises, do you tend to embrace it or avoid it? Do you think I embrace it or avoid it?

FEBRUARY

12

...

Do you ever use humor or sarcasm when you feel uncomfortable in a conversation? Why or why not?

FEBRUARY

13

...

Were your parents affectionate toward each
other when you were a kid? How did you feel
about that?

FEBRUARY

14

...

When was the moment you knew you were in
love with me?

FEBRUARY

15

...

What boundaries can we make that will protect
us from spending too much time on our
phones?

FEBRUARY

16

...

What makes you angry, and what do you do
when you are feeling angry?

FEBRUARY

17

...

Which sex positions are your favorite and why?
Are there any new positions you want to try?

FEBRUARY

18

...

What are the greatest challenges to healthy
communication in relationships in general?

FEBRUARY

19

...

If someone wrote our love story into a book,
what would the title be? Why?

FEBRUARY

20

...

On a scale of 1–10, how important is it to you
to be debt-free? Why is that?

FEBRUARY

21

...

If you could write anything on all of the
billboards of the world for one day, what would
you have them say and why?

FEBRUARY

22

...

Where can you make space in your life to make
sure you have time to recharge?

FEBRUARY

23

...

Who has hurt you the most in your life? What
thoughts and feelings come up when you think
about that person?

FEBRUARY

24

...

What is your favorite adventure that we took
together and why?

FEBRUARY

25

...

In your opinion, what does it mean to be
successful in life?

FEBRUARY

26

...

How would you describe our
communication style?

FEBRUARY

27

...

How do you feel about sexting, phone sex, and
sending each other intimate pictures
throughout the day?

FEBRUARY

28

· · ·

If you could spend your next week anywhere in
the world, where would you go?

FEBRUARY

29

LEAP DAY

· · ·

If you could turn one of your talents into
a career or side business, what would it be
and why?

MARCH

Loving well requires listening well.

MARCH

1

...

What is a topic you think people tend to stay private about and why? Is there a topic you think everyone should be private about?

MARCH

2

...

What are three things that are on your bucket list?

MARCH

3

...

Do you ever feel taken advantage of by those you love? Why or why not?

MARCH

4

. . .

How can we make each other feel more comfortable discussing our sexual likes, preferences, and concerns?

MARCH

5

. . .

Were you allowed to express your emotions as a kid? Why or why not?

MARCH

6

. . .

What is the kindest thing you have ever done for someone?

MARCH

7

· · ·

Do you think that we argue in a healthy way?
Why or why not?

MARCH

8

· · ·

When it comes to your career, do you consider
yourself someone who is confident in their role?
Why or why not?

MARCH

9

· · ·

How can we encourage each other to be more
honest, more vulnerable, and more open when
we have conversations?

MARCH

10
...

What is one bad habit you need to break but do not want to?

MARCH

11
...

How did your parents manage their money when you were growing up? Do you think they did a good job?

MARCH

12
...

What can I do that provides the greatest comfort and encouragement to you when you are hurt, fearful, anxious, or worried?

MARCH

13
...

Which book has had the greatest impact
on your life?

MARCH

14
...

Mindfulness is being present and aware of what
is going on inside you. What are some ways you
can practice mindfulness in your everyday life?

MARCH

15
...

Who are the five people you spend the most
time with? Do you think these people make
your life better?

MARCH
16
...

What is the worst piece of advice anyone has ever given you?

MARCH
17
...

What is an ideal time for us to sit down and talk about our disagreements? Why do you think that works best?

MARCH
18
...

What are two practical ways that I can show my love for you this week?

MARCH

19

...

What do you think is the difference between a lie and a white lie?

MARCH

20

...

What are your thoughts and feelings about masturbation?

MARCH

21

...

What are healthy boundaries that we need to set with our family members to protect our relationship?

MARCH

22

...

What compliment would you really like to hear from me? Why does that mean a lot to you?

MARCH

23

...

Growing up, were you ever left out, bullied, or made fun of by your peers or family members? Explain.

MARCH

24

...

What are your thoughts about cosmetic procedures? Do you think you will ever make any cosmetic changes to your body? Why or why not?

MARCH

25

...

Who taught you about sex? Was it helpful or a
hindrance?

MARCH

26

...

Are there any actions I take that make you feel
like I don't care about you or our relationship?
Explain.

MARCH

27

...

What are your thoughts about therapy or
getting outside help for yourself or our
relationship?

MARCH

28
...

Who do you look up to as an example of a
healthy relationship?

MARCH

29
...

What are some wise financial decisions you
made in the past?

MARCH

30
...

What makes you feel emotionally connected
to me?

MARCH

31

...

How would you like to be held before, during, and after sex?

APRIL

...

*Communication
is what
connects us.*

APRIL

1
...

Looking back at the last month or so, do you think you spent your free time wisely? Why or why not?

APRIL

2
...

When was the last time you felt misunderstood by someone? How did you respond?

APRIL

3
...

What is one failure that has turned into a meaningful lesson for you?

APRIL

4
...

Do you believe that some things in life are
unforgivable? Explain.

APRIL

5
...

What are ways we can make our sexual intimacy
a bigger priority in this season of life?

APRIL

6
...

Who was your childhood hero and why?

APRIL

7

...

Do you tend to be more of an internal or verbal
processor? Have you always been this way?

APRIL

8

...

How do you feel when you are emotionally
exposed and vulnerable with me?

APRIL

9

...

What are two things you love about your job or
career and why?

APRIL

10

...

Have you ever heard any stories about anything
interesting that happened during or soon after
your birth? If so, what happened?

APRIL

11

...

When was the last time you felt vulnerable?
Who were you with and how did you handle the
situation?

APRIL

12

...

Where are three places on your body you like to
be kissed other than your lips?

APRIL

13
...

What are some in-home and casual date ideas
you'd want us to plan?

APRIL

14
...

What's the time that you have laughed the
hardest in your life?

APRIL

15
...

Would you rather win one million dollars today
or ten million dollars in ten years? Why?

APRIL

16

· · ·

What's a common piece of marriage or relationship advice that you don't agree with and why?

APRIL

17

· · ·

How do you deal with disappointments? Is this something you want to work on and why?

APRIL

18

· · ·

What commitments have we been prioritizing over our relationship? (Examples: kids, work, friends, social media, family, technology, etc.)

APRIL

19

...

Are there any feelings or thoughts that get in the way of me giving you oral sex? Why or why not?

APRIL

20

...

What are you most grateful for in this season of your life and why?

APRIL

21

...

Do you ever struggle with interrupting others? How do you think interrupting affects a conversation?

APRIL

22

...

Growing up, did you watch your parents lie to each other? Did your parents ever lie to you?

APRIL

23

...

What is your current favorite TV show, movie, and app and why?

APRIL

24

...

Who is someone you know who is very defensive? Were they always like this? Do you think they're aware of how they come across?

APRIL

25

...

How do our differences help us complement
each other?

APRIL

26

...

What are your thoughts and feelings about
scheduling sex?

APRIL

27

...

Of all the people that you know personally, who
would make the best president? Why?

APRIL

28

...

At what age do you want to retire and what type of lifestyle do you want to lead in retirement?

APRIL

29

...

Do people often ask for your help with something specific? What is that thing and why do you think they ask you and not someone else?

APRIL

30

...

Have I done anything in the last month that has caused you pain? How did that make you feel?

MAY

Open your mind before you open your mouth.

MAY

1

...

In your opinion, what are some qualities of a
good listener?

MAY

2

...

Was there anything your parents or siblings said
that really hurt and that you still remember to
this day? Why or why not?

MAY

3

...

What have you done in your life that you are
most proud of and why?

MAY

4
...

How would you like to financially invest in our relationship? (Examples: date nights, weekend getaways, therapy, reading more marriage books, couple retreats, etc.)

MAY

5
...

What exactly does an orgasm feel like to you?

MAY

6
...

In what ways do our arguments and hard experiences help us grow as a couple?

MAY

7

...

When making a decision, do you tend to rely on logic, emotions, or both? Which do you think should have the final say?

MAY

8

...

Is there anything that makes you feel uncomfortable about my parents and family? Why or why not?

MAY

9

...

Do you believe in second chances? Why or why not?

MAY

10

...

What household chore have you never done but
probably should?

MAY

11

...

Have any of your friendships become strained
or distant over time? Why do you think that is?

MAY

12

...

Where are two places you would like to make
love other than in our bed?

MAY

13

• • •

In your opinion, what are some qualities of a
best friend?

MAY

14

• • •

What are your biggest worries about the
future? Is there anything I can do to support
you?

MAY

15

• • •

Have you ever expressed your feelings and been
met with judgment or criticism or been
ignored? What happened?

MAY

16

· · ·

What is the most memorable gift you ever
received?

MAY

17

· · ·

With all of the conversations we've had in the
last few months, what have you learned about
us, yourself, and me?

MAY

18

· · ·

What are some ways your parents showed their
love for you while you were growing up?

MAY

19

...

How many times have you been in love?
Tell me about it.

MAY

20

...

What are some things that stress you out when
talking about money?

MAY

21

...

When it comes to sex, do you like it when I am
in control, or do you prefer to take the lead?
Why?

MAY

22

. . .

What are some behaviors that you think should
never be tolerated in our relationship and why?

MAY

23

. . .

When was a time in your life that trust was
broken and it made a big impact on you?

MAY

24

. . .

If you could come up with one word that sums
up this season of your life, what would it be?
Why did you choose that word?

MAY

25
...

What are two things you can do regularly to
reduce stress?

MAY

26
...

Do you consider yourself to be more of a
hoarder, a minimalist, or somewhere in
between? Were you always this way?

MAY

27
...

When it comes to your sex drive, do you feel
like you have a high, average, or low libido
and why?

MAY

28

· · ·

How would you like us to celebrate your
birthday and our anniversary?

MAY

29

· · ·

In your opinion, which characteristics make
someone reliable? Do you think you are
reliable?

MAY

30

· · ·

If you could make one rule that everyone had to
follow, what would it be?

What are some activities and adventures you
want to plan for the summer?

JUNE
. . .

*Never stop learning
how to love each other.*

JUNE

1

...

Are there any unresolved conflicts or issues that we need to address that are standing in the way of our having fun together? If so, what are they?

JUNE

2

...

How confident are you in your abilities to make decisions for yourself? Have you always been this way?

JUNE

3

...

How can we verbally express satisfaction during foreplay and sex?

JUNE

4

...

Do you struggle with comparison? Who do you compare yourself to and how does that impact you?

JUNE

5

...

Do you think our current work-life dynamic is working for our relationship? Why or why not?

JUNE

6

...

Why do you believe some people get stuck in their ways and never change their behaviors?

JUNE

7

...

In your opinion, what does it look like to be financially prepared for an emergency?

JUNE

8

...

What are two negative behaviors that your parents modeled? Did they ever apologize for them?

JUNE

9

...

Do you feel like you are assertive with me often, sometimes, or rarely? Have you always been this way, or has it changed over time?

JUNE

10
. . .

What outfit do you think I look sexiest in and why?

JUNE

11
. . .

Do you ever struggle with overscheduling and overplanning to keep busy? Why or why not?

JUNE

12
. . .

When was the last time you tried something for the first time?

JUNE

13
· · ·

Do any of my friends make you feel uncomfortable? Is there any boundary we need to discuss regarding this friendship?

JUNE

14
· · ·

What three qualities about me were you first attracted to?

JUNE

15
· · ·

When you were growing up, how did your parents handle conflict with each other?

JUNE

16

. . .

Do you consider yourself someone who gets
embarrassed easily? Why or why not?

JUNE

17

. . .

How do you see our sex life changing through
the years?

JUNE

18

. . .

What are three things that bore you?

How did we make each other smile this week?

What are some tangible things I can do to show
you that I'm someone you can rely on?

Are there any topics or situations that put you
in a bad mood? (Examples: the news, politics,
traffic, a bad night's sleep, work, etc.) Why do
you think that is?

JUNE

22

...

What summer traditions did you experience as a
kid that you loved and why?

JUNE

23

...

When we work together on our budget and
financial goals, how does it make you feel?

JUNE

24

...

What is an erotic thing I can do in the bedroom
that you would enjoy?

JUNE

25

...

Do you think that your parents and family show you respect? Why or why not?

JUNE

26

...

Do you ever feel guilty for spending time on yourself and why?

JUNE

27

...

Do you tend to be impulsive when making decisions? Why or why not?

JUNE

28

· · ·

What is the most adventurous thing you've ever
done? Would you want to do it again?

JUNE

29

· · ·

How comfortable are you with showing
affection in public? Have you always felt
this way?

JUNE

30

· · ·

Who is a person you trust enough to seek
relationship advice from and why? What makes
this person trustworthy?

JULY

7

...

Work on your relationship every single day, not just during the hard times.

JULY

1
...

Who is someone that gives you anxiety? What
do they do that makes you anxious?

JULY

2
...

What is your favorite date that we have ever
been on? What made it special to you?

JULY

3
...

What is your favorite part of our foreplay? Is
there anything different you would like to try?

JULY

4
...

If you could trade places with any person right
now, who would it be and why?

JULY

5
...

Did your parents model and teach you about
healthy boundaries? If so, how?

JULY

6
...

Were there any red flags you saw in past
relationships that you ignored? Why do you
think that was?

JULY

7
...

What one thing do you really want to purchase
but can't afford yet?

JULY

8
...

When you are going through a difficult time,
who can you go to for honest feedback and
support to help you process what you're going
through?

JULY

9
...

Are you someone who is quick to apologize?
Why or why not?

JULY

10
· · ·

Growing up, did you ever feel neglected or
overlooked by your parents? Why or why not?

JULY

11
· · ·

What goal have you been putting off recently?
Why?

JULY

12
· · ·

Do you prefer to have sex in the morning, the
afternoon, or the evening? Why?

JULY

13

· · ·

What do you think is your biggest struggle with communication? What is one thing you can do to start working on that?

JULY

14

· · ·

Is cooking together something you'd want to try? Are there any recipes you want to cook together?

JULY

15

· · ·

Do you feel like you have control over your emotions most of the time? Why or why not?

JULY

16

. . .

Which ten words would you use to describe yourself?

JULY

17

. . .

If you could pick one year of your life to do over, which year would it be and why?

JULY

18

. . .

Did your parents ever talk to you about work ethic, workaholism, the importance of being a hard worker, etc.? How did this affect you?

JULY

19

...

If you could be wildly talented at one thing, what would you choose?

JULY

20

...

What are some ways you would like to have more fun in our relationship? (Examples: date nights, adventures, road trips, sex, board games, etc.)

JULY

21

...

How do you think your upbringing affects your views on sex and intimacy?

JULY

22

...

In your opinion, what is the difference between failing and being a failure?

JULY

23

...

How soon after an argument are you willing to be intimate? What are your thoughts about "make up sex"?

JULY

24

...

Is social media bringing us closer or making us more isolated? Why do you think that is?

25

...

When you were a child, what was the biggest lie
you ever told? Did you ever get caught?

26

...

Do you think you show me empathy often,
sometimes, or rarely and why?

27

...

Are there any financial investments you would
like to make in the future? Explain.

JULY

28

...

What are your thoughts about couples counseling? Do you think there have been times when it would have helped our relationship?

JULY

29

...

What areas in our life have gotten in the way of making our physical intimacy a priority?

JULY

30

...

Who do you know, from the past or present, that has a healthy and happy relationship? What do you think makes that relationship strong?

31

...

If you could spend a day talking to one person,
alive or dead, who would it be and why?

AUGUST

. . .

Communication is about how you talk and how you listen.

AUGUST

1

...

When in your life have you hurt someone close to you? What happened?

AUGUST

2

...

What is one area of your life you can work on decluttering? (Examples: the house, social media, your schedule, emails, etc.)

AUGUST

3

...

Are you someone who spends a lot of time in deep thought, processing things before making a decision, or do you tend to make quick decisions? Why or why not?

AUGUST

4

...

Do you enjoy running errands?
Why or why not?

AUGUST

5

...

What is one thing you would like to change
about yourself and why?

AUGUST

6

...

What makes our relationship special or unique
compared with that of others we know?

AUGUST

7
...

If your past boyfriends or girlfriends listed out all of your positive traits, what would they say?

AUGUST

8
...

Share a time when you felt truly understood and prioritized. What emotions did you feel?

AUGUST

9
...

What is your secret sexual fantasy? How long have you been fantasizing about it?

AUGUST

10

...

If you had to be on a reality TV show, which one
would you be on and why?

AUGUST

11

...

What are some boundaries you have put in
place that you are proud of?

AUGUST

12

...

Do you feel like you have a healthy relationship
with alcohol? Why or why not?

AUGUST

13

...

How often do you think about money and finances? How does it make you feel to think about money?

AUGUST

14

...

What are your thoughts about us being active together? Is there any form of exercise you want to try together? Why?

AUGUST

15

...

Did your parents express anger? If so, how?

AUGUST

16

...

What is something you can do today but were
not capable of doing ten years ago?

AUGUST

17

...

How important are anniversaries, Valentine's
Day, and birthdays to you? Is there any specific
way you like to celebrate these holidays?

AUGUST

18

...

As a couple, what are some heated or sensitive
topics we need to be aware of that usually turn
discussion into conflict?

AUGUST

19

. . .

Does thinking about the future scare or
excite you? Why?

AUGUST

20

. . .

If you could talk to your teenage self, what
would you say?

AUGUST

21

. . .

If our house were on fire and you knew that our
family members and pets were safe, what things
would you want to rescue from the fire?

AUGUST

22
...

When it comes to our daily chores and responsibilities, do you feel like things are fair or does something need to change? Why or why not?

AUGUST

23
...

As a couple, how can we give back to others, or to our community, in a way that we are not currently doing?

AUGUST

24
...

How does it make you feel when you bring me to orgasm?

AUGUST

25
...

On a scale of 1–10, how comfortable are you with expressing your feelings? (10 = very comfortable and 1 = not comfortable at all)

AUGUST

26
...

What are the topics we will *not* discuss with our parents and family members? (Examples: our sex life, money, parenting, past arguments, etc.)

AUGUST

27
...

What could I say and do to make you feel respected?

AUGUST

28

· · ·

What is one financial decision you made in the
past that you regret?

AUGUST

29

· · ·

Do you ever find that you compare our life to
what you watch on TV or see online?

AUGUST

30

· · ·

Do you feel like your parents made their
relationship a priority? What did that look like?

31

...

How can we add more spontaneity, creativity,
and romance in the bedroom?

SEPTEMBER

*All relationships,
no matter how good,
can be made better.*

SEPTEMBER

1

...

What does your dream house
look like?

SEPTEMBER

2

...

What is something you did or didn't do today
that you would love to do every day?
Why is that?

SEPTEMBER

3

...

Looking back at our past conflicts, what have
you learned about yourself? What have you
learned about our relationship?

SEPTEMBER

4

...

Do you think our schedules are causing stress
and exhaustion? Why?

SEPTEMBER

5

...

What new tradition or ritual do you want us to
start in our relationship?

SEPTEMBER

6

...

What do you love about your personality? Have
you always felt this way?

SEPTEMBER

7

What have you enjoyed about our sex life in the
last couple of months?

SEPTEMBER

8

What are some behaviors or actions that you
consider cheating or crossing a line?

SEPTEMBER

9

...

Do you consider yourself a saver, a spender, or a
little of both? Have you always been this way
and do you wish you were different?

SEPTEMBER
10
...

When you were growing up, did you feel like your parents and family members respected each other often, sometimes, or rarely? How did they show it?

SEPTEMBER
11
...

What is a loss that you've experienced in your life? Do you feel like you were able to go through the grieving process?

SEPTEMBER
12
...

What makes you feel the most insecure? How do you handle your insecurities?

SEPTEMBER

13

...

What areas of our relationship do we need to
talk more about, even if it's uncomfortable?

SEPTEMBER

14

...

What are your thoughts about meal planning
and sticking to a grocery budget?

SEPTEMBER

15

...

Has the tone of my voice ever affected (either
positively or negatively) a conversation we've
had? Tell me more.

SEPTEMBER

16

· · ·

Would you rather have a noisy neighbor or a
nosy neighbor? Why?

SEPTEMBER

17

· · ·

Do you consider yourself an open book or more
of a private person? Were you always this way?

SEPTEMBER

18

· · ·

What are some things you do to have fun while
I'm not around?

SEPTEMBER

19

...

Do you ever struggle to trust me? What can I do to help rebuild trust in our relationship?

SEPTEMBER

20

...

What is one of your guilty pleasures?

SEPTEMBER

21

...

What thoughts come to your mind when thinking of the quote "Hurt people hurt people"?

SEPTEMBER

22
· · ·

What are three of your best childhood
memories with your family? What makes those
memories stand out to you?

SEPTEMBER

23
· · ·

What is one area that I can work on when it
comes to money and our relationship?

SEPTEMBER

24
· · ·

How can I show that I am sexually attracted
to you?

SEPTEMBER

25

· · ·

How often do you say yes to something and
regret it—often, sometimes, or rarely? Why?

SEPTEMBER

26

· · ·

Is there anyone in our lives who talks negatively
about others often? How do you tend to engage
with them? Is that healthy?

SEPTEMBER

27

· · ·

What is your favorite way to relax when things
are hectic?

SEPTEMBER

28

...

In your opinion, what qualities does a healthy
relationship have?

SEPTEMBER

29

...

If we ran a business together, what would it be?

SEPTEMBER

30

...

What were some ways we connected
emotionally this last month that you enjoyed?

OCTOBER

10
· · ·

The more you talk about your thoughts and feelings, the more comfortable it becomes.

OCTOBER

1

...

What are some ways we can make sure we are more present and less distracted when we're spending time together?

OCTOBER

2

...

Have you ever felt judged, ignored, or mistreated because of your race? Why or why not?

OCTOBER

3

...

When was the last time you cried? What did you cry about?

OCTOBER

4
...

What are some ways I can help around the house this week?

OCTOBER

5
...

If a movie were being made about us, who would play you and me? What would the storyline be about?

OCTOBER

6
...

When you make a mistake, how do you react? Are you hard on yourself or do you give yourself grace? Have you always been this way?

OCTOBER

7

...

If you could have the credit for creating any piece of art (a painting, music, movie, etc.), which piece of art would you choose and why?

OCTOBER

8

...

What are two positive patterns or beliefs that your parents taught you as a child?

OCTOBER

9

...

Is there anyone or anything in your life right now that is causing you to feel depressed or insecure? Why or why not?

OCTOBER

10

. . .

What's the most romantic thing I've ever done
for you? Would you want me to do it again
and why?

OCTOBER

11

. . .

Do you feel like you watch a healthy amount of
TV or too much? Why do you think that is?

OCTOBER

12

. . .

Do you appreciate love letters and encouraging
notes? If so, how often would you like me to
write them for you?

OCTOBER

13
...

What is something you've always felt was
missing from your life?

OCTOBER

14
...

What are some shared goals or projects we can
work on together to strengthen our bond?

OCTOBER

15
...

How do you handle disappointment with
others? (Examples: I get angry, I withdraw, I
ignore, I cry, I try to numb the pain, etc.)

OCTOBER
16
...

What would you like to be known for, both personally and professionally?

OCTOBER
17
...

How do you feel about the pace of your life? Is it too fast, too slow, or just about right?

OCTOBER
18
...

What are ways we can be more intentional with making time for fun as individuals and as a couple?

OCTOBER

19
...

What is your favorite romantic song for us to
play in the bedroom and why?

OCTOBER

20
...

If you died tomorrow, what would your friends
and family say about you at your funeral?

OCTOBER

21
...

What amount of money would we have to earn
to make us feel financially secure in our life
together?

OCTOBER

22

. . .

How does stress affect your body? How do you
think it affects our relationship?

OCTOBER

23

. . .

What are your thoughts and feelings about
sharing passwords with each other?

OCTOBER

24

. . .

What are things we can both do to create a safe
and caring environment for us to disagree
without allowing it to escalate?

OCTOBER

25

. . .

Based on our personal experiences, what advice
would you give someone who is dating?

OCTOBER

26

. . .

When I sense that you're upset or acting
differently, what is the best way for me to bring
this up so we can have a healthy conversation?

OCTOBER

27

. . .

What is something you did not want to do at all
that turned out to be a great experience?

OCTOBER

28

...

When you got in trouble as a kid, how did your parents discipline you?

OCTOBER

29

...

What role does kissing play during foreplay and sex?

OCTOBER

30

...

On a scale of 1–10, what is the highest level of pain you have ever felt? What happened?

OCTOBER

31

...

What was your favorite Halloween costume as a
kid and why?

11
NOVEMBER
...

Just as a tree needs water and sunlight, a relationship needs good communication and love to grow and thrive.

NOVEMBER

1

...

When was the most difficult time of your life?
How do you think that has affected you?

NOVEMBER

2

...

What is a new holiday tradition you want to
start this year?

NOVEMBER

3

...

Is there anything I need to apologize for that
has chipped away at your trust of me?

NOVEMBER

4
...

If you were given one million dollars, what would you spend it on and why?

NOVEMBER

5
...

What do you wish you could tell the you of five years ago?

NOVEMBER

6
...

If you were in charge of the country for one week, what is one thing you would do?

NOVEMBER

7

...

If you could change anything about the way you were raised, what would it be and why?

NOVEMBER

8

...

What are you most excited for this holiday season?

NOVEMBER

9

...

On the days when we do not have much time for sex, what are some ways that I can help you get in the mood quicker and make it enjoyable?

NOVEMBER

10
...

What are three things you wish were different
with your job or career and why?

NOVEMBER

11
...

What are things I do that make you feel
connected and cared for?

NOVEMBER

12
...

What are some boundaries we need to set
regarding our exes?

NOVEMBER

13

...

What are some mistakes you made in past relationships that you regret?

NOVEMBER

14

...

What is your idea of the perfect date night?

NOVEMBER

15

...

What are some areas that you want to protect and prioritize for your mental health and why?

NOVEMBER

16

. . .

What is one strange habit you have that most
people do not know about?

NOVEMBER

17

. . .

Is there anything you would like me to do to
you sexually that I haven't done yet? Why or
why not?

NOVEMBER

18

. . .

Growing up, what were your favorite
Thanksgiving traditions?

NOVEMBER

19

· · ·

Is there anything I can do to help you feel
emotionally safe to share your thoughts and
feelings with me?

NOVEMBER

20

· · ·

Do you consider yourself someone who is
handy around the house? Why or why not?

NOVEMBER

21

· · ·

What is something adventurous you have always
wanted to experience?

NOVEMBER

22

...

How do the differences in our personality traits impact our communication? (Examples: introversion and extroversion, optimism and pessimism, thinking and feeling, etc.)

NOVEMBER

23

...

What is something, or someone, that always makes you laugh or smile and why?

NOVEMBER

24

...

How could we be generous to others this holiday season?

NOVEMBER

25

...

If you could have a second chance at one event of your life, what would you choose? What would you do differently?

NOVEMBER

26

...

When you were crying or upset, how did your parents soothe and comfort you emotionally?

NOVEMBER

27

...

When you were growing up, did your family encourage and value therapy? Why do you think that was?

NOVEMBER

28

...

Are you more of a detail person or a big-picture person? Have you always been this way?

NOVEMBER

29

...

Are there any charitable foundations or nonprofits you would like to give to financially and why?

NOVEMBER

30

...

Are you able to recognize when you're emotionally triggered or upset? Why or why not?

DECEMBER

The best gift you can give your partner is time.

DECEMBER

1

...

What are some ways that we can ensure we are spending quality time together this holiday season?

DECEMBER

2

...

What is your favorite way to learn? Listening to podcasts, reading, taking online classes, watching documentaries, or something else?

DECEMBER

3

...

What do you hope for in the next year of our relationship?

DECEMBER

4

...

If you didn't have to work, what would you do with your time?

DECEMBER

5

...

What is your best advice for someone who has lost hope?

DECEMBER

6

...

Which of our past sexual experiences have been your favorite and why?

DECEMBER
7
· · ·

When you come home from work, what can I do or say that will make you feel the most loved?

DECEMBER
8
· · ·

What are some things that stress you out about the holiday season? (Examples: crowded stores, seeing relatives, spending money, pressures at work, etc.)

DECEMBER
9
· · ·

What are some things I can do or say to communicate I understand your views, feelings, and opinions?

DECEMBER
10
...

What small wins did you experience this week?

DECEMBER
11
...

Do you tend to meet others' needs before your own? Why or why not?

DECEMBER
12
...

What are some ways that the internet and social media have changed the way people communicate with each other?

DECEMBER

13
...

What is the best Christmas gift you ever
received?

DECEMBER

14
...

In your opinion, what is the difference between
a sincere and an insincere apology?

DECEMBER

15
...

What are your thoughts about lending money
to family members or friends?

DECEMBER

16

. . .

If you could whisk us away for a romantic
getaway, where would it be and why?

DECEMBER

17

. . .

What was your first job? What did it teach you
about work ethic, earning money, and working
with others?

DECEMBER

18

. . .

Growing up, what were your favorite
Christmas traditions?

DECEMBER

19

• • •

Do you feel like stress has impacted your libido at any point in our relationship? Why or why not?

DECEMBER

20

• • •

What do you believe is one of the greatest inventions ever created and why?

DECEMBER

21

• • •

Do you think our upbringings and how we saw our parents communicate were similar or different? How do you think that affects us today?

DECEMBER

22

...

Do you believe in love at first sight? Why or
why not?

DECEMBER

23

...

What is your favorite holiday movie and why?

DECEMBER

24

...

Are you someone who likes surprises or do they
unsettle you? Why or why not?

DECEMBER

25

• • •

If you had five million dollars to give away, what would you do with it to impact the most people?

DECEMBER

26

• • •

What is something I do and could do more that helps you feel validated in your feelings?

DECEMBER

27

• • •

What are some dreams and desires that you want to accomplish at some point?

DECEMBER

28

. . .

What did you want to be when you were a kid
and why?

DECEMBER

29

. . .

How did you find out there was no Santa Claus,
Easter Bunny, or tooth fairy?

DECEMBER

30

. . .

What are your thoughts about New Year's
resolutions? Have you ever made and kept one?

31
...

How would you feel if your life and our relationship looked exactly the same in five years?

BONUS MONTH

Give your partner your undivided attention.

1. What causes and movements are you passionate about?

2. What is the biggest challenge you face when you try to meet personal goals?

3. What is a situation that puts you in a bad mood?

4. When you feel alone in our relationship or upset by life, what are your go-to's to help numb the pain? (Examples: TV, alcohol, reading, eating, porn, shopping, video games, etc.)

5. What is an area (or topic) of our communication that we do really well?

6. What were some ways we had fun while we were dating and engaged?

7. In your opinion, what do you think is the biggest struggle kids are going through that we never had to deal with growing up?

8. Have you ever taken any kind of personality assessment? If so, which ones? Did you agree with the results?

9. What lie do you tell yourself most often?

10. Which kinds of actions and words cause you to feel disrespected by others?

11. Do you feel like you can easily view a situation from someone else's perspective? Why or why not?

12. Which area of your life is in the most need of healthy boundaries and why? (Examples: work, schedules, tech, etc.)

13. When was the last time you were told no? How did it happen, and what did it teach you?

14. Growing up, did you feel emotionally safe to speak up and ask your parents anything? Why or why not?

15. What are you most proud of in our relationship? Why is that?

16. What is the most meaningful thing we have accomplished together?

17. When do you need assurance of my love the most and why?

18. What is one part of your daily routine that you'd probably be better off not doing and why?

19. When you face challenges, do you feel overwhelmed and hopeless or empowered and excited? Why?

20. What would you like to stop worrying about? What steps can you take to let go of the worry?

21. When are you the most inspired, most motivated, and most charged up?

22. What is your moral compass for making difficult decisions?

23. In what ways has our relationship changed you?

24. What issue do most people think is black-and-white but you think has a lot of nuance?

25. What is something you are self-conscious about? Have you always felt this way?

26. What beliefs do you have about yourself that resulted from your childhood?

27. What is something that is true for you no matter what?

28. What would you do if you woke up to find yourself completely invisible?

29. How can you begin to find joy in what you have right now instead of focusing on what you don't yet have?

30. What are some barriers that keep you from apologizing when you have made a mistake? (Examples: pride, shame, fear, doubt, rejection, etc.)

31. What is the earliest memory that you can recall? Tell me about it.

BONUS SECTION #1: FOR PARENTS

1. How would you describe your parenting style? Do you like your parenting style?

2. What do you think your greatest strength as a parent is and why?

3. Do you think our children would say we are a fun family? Why or why not?

4. Who in our life do you think is a good role model for our children? What kind of character traits do they have?

5. What do you miss most about your life pre-kids?

6. What are some of your greatest fears about raising our children?

7. In ten years, where would you like to see our family live? Why?

8. Do you think we should give our kids an allowance? Why or why not?

9. How involved do you want our kids' grandparents to be in our parenting and family life?

10. What are your thoughts about homeschooling, private school, and public school for our children?

11. Do you think you are strict, soft, or somewhere in between with our kids? Do you think this is effective and why?

12. What are your thoughts on teaching our kids about anatomy and sex? Do you feel prepared for this conversation? Does it ever make you feel nervous or anxious?

13. What are some ideas for having more fun with our children? Are there any activities or games you'd like to try?

14. What are some values you think are important to our family and why?

15. In twenty years, where would you like to see our family financially?

16. If we had a family motto, in one sentence, what would it be?

17. Do you think our kids know that we love each other? What do you think they notice about our interactions?

18. What is one thing you would want others to say about our family? (Examples: that we are kind, generous, forgiving, hardworking, loyal, fun, etc.)

19. Do you think our family would ever benefit from family counseling? Why?

20. What age would you say our kids can start dating and why?

21. Which of our children need some extra love and attention right now? How can we make this happen?

22. Is there anything you want to teach our children regarding faith and spirituality?

23. What do you want to improve when it comes to parenting our children?

24. What are some of the boundaries you think we should implement with our kids and their screen time?

25. Do you think our kids know how to face their fears, feelings, and conflict, or do you think they tend to avoid them? Do you think we have ever modeled avoidance?

26. What have our kids learned about communication from watching us interact with each other? Is this something we need to improve and why?

27. What are some ways we can incorporate more meaningful conversations with our kids into our day-to-day lives?

28. What are some ways we can teach our children to save their money, budget, and not get into financial debt?

29. What are some ways we can encourage our children to be generous with their money? Are there any nonprofits or organizations we can give to as a family and invite the kids to be part of it?

30. What are we doing to teach our kids about how to handle disappointment? Do you think they know how to communicate their expectations to others?

31. Do you think we ever expect too much from our children? Why or why not?

32. What are some ways we can teach our kids to be hard workers and have a healthy work ethic?

33. What can we do to show our children that our family is the safest place in their lives?

34. What are some ways we can teach our kids to have a healthy view of sex?

35. Looking back, what was the hardest thing about the transition from being a couple to being parents?

36. What have been some challenges since becoming a parent? (Examples: sleep deprivation, loss of identity, feeling that life is now mundane, loss of independence, exhaustion, loneliness, etc.)

37. How can we support each other through this time of parenting and all of the demands that come with it?

38. We know that it takes a village to raise children. Do you ever feel uncomfortable or guilty for asking others for help? Why or why not?

39. When you think about our buckets of time ("me time," family time, couple time), which bucket needs a little more attention and why?

40. What are some practical ways we can make sure both of us have time for self-care?

41. What are some ways we can make sure we keep our emotional connection strong and alive while raising our kids?

42. When our children become emotionally flooded, what is something we can do to help them calm down and work through their emotions?

43. How can we model and talk about emotions with our children? Do we allow ourselves to show our true emotions with them and why?

44. How can we teach our children to admit their mistakes and work on earning back trust with their friends and siblings when they've let someone down?

45. Recently, do you think I've given you my best or my left-overs? Is this an area you think I could improve in?

46. As parents, how can we model for our kids what healthy conflict looks like?

47. What do you think is the hardest thing about this season of raising our kids?

48. What kind of grandparents do you think we'll be?

49. What has parenting taught you about yourself? About life in general?

50. Who should pay for our kids' college? Us, them, or a little of both?

51. What is one thing you think we should apologize to the kids for?

52. What can we do to ensure that when the kids leave the home and we become empty nesters, we still have a strong connection in our marriage?

BONUS SECTION #2: FAITH AND SPIRITUALITY

1. What role do faith and spirituality play in your life? Were you raised in a faith tradition?

2. Do you believe in God and if so how did you come to that view?

3. What is your perspective on sharing your faith with others?

4. What are the last three spiritual books you've read?

5. Who is your spiritual hero and why?

6. How does prayer play a role in your day-to-day life?

7. How and when do you feel most connected with God?

8. How important is it for you to belong to a local church or other religious gathering place?

9. What are some of the religious values your family celebrates?

10. What are your feelings toward giving to a church or other charitable organizations?

11. What qualities do you consider a person with spiritual peace to have?

12. What is your view on how much people should be involved in their spiritual community?

13. What do you love most about your church or faith community?

14. When you are struggling through something in life, what do you think God wants you to learn from it?

15. What do you imagine the afterlife will be like?

16. Where do you find yourself in your relationship with God right now? Are you happy with where you stand with him and why?

17. Do you feel like God is listening to your prayers lately? Why or why not?

18. When do you feel most distant from God and why?

19. What are some ways we can make prayer and devotion a part of our daily routine, as individuals and as a couple?

20. What is something God created on Earth that still amazes you and why?

21. When you get to the afterlife and can talk to God, what is the first thing you are going to ask him?

22. What specific prayers, big or small, has God answered recently?

23. What is a scripture that brings you peace and why?

24. How can we grow together in our faith, and what steps can we take to make that happen?

25. Was there ever a time you believed God spoke to you? Why or why not?

26. Have you ever been angry at God? Why or why not?

27. Have you ever felt disappointed with God? Why or why not?

28. Do you feel like you expect too much from God at times? Or do you feel like you are expecting too little from him? Why do you feel that way?

29. What are some ways we can pray for each other daily?

30. Do you have a regular worship practice? How important is singing to God for you, and why?

31. What are some spiritual verses that inspire us as a couple, and how can we apply them to our relationship?

32. What are some ways we can better support each other in our spiritual journeys?

33. What is one small thing that you feel God is asking you to do this week?

34. What is one thing that you can do today that will help you feel closer to God?

35. What are five things that God has blessed you with this last year?

36. Do you feel like you're using all the talents God gave you? Why or why not?

37. Is there anything in your spiritual journey that you're only doing because other people told you that you should? Why or why not?

38. Have you ever questioned if God was real? Why or why not?

39. What can you tell me about anyone in your life who claimed to have faith but did not live it out?

40. How have you seen God provide for you financially over the years?

41. Is there any other religion you have been curious to learn about? Why or why not?

42. What do you think separates people who believe in God from those who do not?

43. How do you discern between God speaking to you and your own thoughts?

44. Do you believe that God brought us together? Why or why not?

45. Who in our lives should we be praying for this week?

ACKNOWLEDGMENTS

We want to thank Lucinda Halpern, who believed in our mission and us from day one. Thank you for fighting for us, laughing with us, and being the perfect mixture of truth and love. We literally wouldn't be here without you.

To our Marriage365 staff: You are the BEST people to work alongside and it's your hard work and creativity that have helped the mission of Marriage365 continue. While we may be the founders, you all are the backbone.

Liz Morrow—to work with a husband-and-wife team with strong opinions is not an easy task but you do it so well and with so much patience. Thank you for taking our ideas and making them readable!

ABOUT MARRIAGE365

Just three years into marriage, if you'd asked anyone who knew us personally, we'd have been voted the couple least likely to succeed. We literally hated each other and had no idea how to get back the love and connection we'd once felt. Through lots of stumbling and trial and error, we did manage to walk back from the brink of divorce. But it was incredibly hard. Largely because there were no affordable and accessible resources for us back then. We felt like we were fumbling around in the dark.

So we created the exact resource we wish we'd had: Marriage365. Our restored marriage was the inspiration to help other couples who were feeling stuck, lost, and confused about how to reconnect. Today, our app and website reach millions of couples around the world every day, providing practical advice, tools, and inspiration. You can find all of those resources at marriage365.com. Our mission is to create a safe place for people to grow and ask questions that is available to anyone. Money or privilege should never prevent someone from getting the tools they need to better themselves and their relationships.

We also learned along the journey that the best way to improve those relationships is to become the best version of yourself. If you want to be a better partner, spouse, friend, or parent, become a better you. That's how you experience the true power of connection in your relationships.

We have a dream to see every couple who picks up this

book become happy, connected, and understood by each other. It's what gets us up every morning. Our life's work is to help build healthy relationships and bring hope to those who desire to live to the fullest. We want Marriage365 to become the most trusted and available resource for relationship advice.

Take it from us, if we can build a healthy relationship, so can you. We're far from perfect and have to take our own advice all the time. We still use this book almost every single day. Yes, the questions we wrote for you are the ones we ask each other regularly. After a long day of work and parenting, we don't have the creative energy to come up with interesting topics of conversation. We take this book on every date night and ask each other the same questions we have been for years. Because just like us, the answers change. There's no shame in needing tools to help you. These 365+ questions are still foundational to our connection and relationship. This stuff works; we promise.

ABOUT THE AUTHORS

Casey and **Meygan Caston** are the co-founders of Marriage365 and are committed to helping couples and individuals become healthy and happy. They reach millions of people worldwide with vulnerability by sharing their stories of struggle and success. Casey and Meygan live in Orange County, California, with their two kids, where you can find them at the beach, walking their dog, taking cold plunges, and playing Sudoku.

BONUS QUESTION

Are you searching for new ways to strengthen your connection with your spouse? Look no further than **Marriage365**. Join the thriving community of over 100,000 couples who are committed to enhancing their marriages together.

Discover a World of Connection:

 Explore thousands of Connecting Questions designed to deepen your understanding of each other.

 Dive into a treasure trove of instructional videos, podcasts, self-paced courses, and engaging worksheets recommended by experts and therapists.

Unlock the Benefits of Marriage365:

 Elevate communication, intimacy, and conflict resolution with practical lessons and solutions.

 Access relatable resources to tackle common marriage challenges and build a more fulfilling relationship.

 Revitalize your sex life and intimacy with your partner.

To start your **free trial,**
visit **Marriage365.com** or
download the app on your mobile device.